The Lazy Dog's Guide
to Enlightenment

Andrea Hurst and Beth Wilson
Foreword by Dr. Bernie S. Siegel
Photographs by Zachary Folk

The LAZY DOG'S Guide
to ENLIGHTENMENT

New World Library
Novato, California

New World Library
14 Pamaron Way
Novato, California 94949

Edited by Vanessa Brown and Kristen Cashman
Text design and typography by Mary Ann Casler

Library of Congress Cataloging-in-Publication Data is available upon request.

First printing, April 2007
ISBN-10: 1-57731-571-5
ISBN-13: 978-1-57731-571-1
Printed in China

New World Library is a proud member of the Green Press Initiative.

Distributed by Publishers Group West

10   9   8   7   6   5   4   3   2   1

This book is dedicated to a wonderful whippet named Devo. He was a great friend and my favorite muse. He taught me of the brilliant quirks and beautiful complexities that a canine can possess. I am thankful for all the hours he endured of me trying to capture him on film. He is dearly missed. — Zac

We would like to dedicate this book to the special dogs who have touched our lives: Penny, Keeper, Willow, Lucy, and Ruby. And to the extraordinary dogs everywhere, past, present, and future. — Beth and Andrea

FOREWORD

Perhaps it is no coincidence that the word *dog* spelled backward is *god*. If we observe man's best friend from a new perspective, we may just gain some important wisdom from our canine friends. Dogs can serve as role models for us in many ways. Whenever someone asks me to suggest a role model, I point to my dogs. When I am in doubt about what to do, I ask myself, "WWLD?" Yes, that's "What Would Lassie Do?" You may laugh, but I am serious about this, and so are many others. I also believe dogs are complete in ways we can only aspire to. Completeness is not just about the physical body, but about who we are. There are a lot of amputee dogs named Tripod who are complete beings of love and service.

My wife, Bobbie, and I have five children, all of whom are now grown and have gone off to live their own lives. To help fill the empty nest, we now have two dogs. When I first brought Furphy home, we already had four cats. My wife complained that she didn't want any more "furphys" on the furniture. Is it worth the fur on the furniture, the noise and accidents, and whatever other surprises these dog-beings bring into our lives? Yes! Our second dog came to us in a special way. I had just written a short story about a dog and named him Buddy. On my next visit to our local animal shelter I met an abandoned dog and his name was Buddy. I accepted God's will and brought my new friend home.

These characters have become a part of our family and a part of our personal history. They live in the house with us; they sit and sleep together with us. They have brought something unique and satisfying to our lives. They have loved us unconditionally and have taught us important lessons for better living — how to embrace life, how to enjoy the moment, how to let go when it's time to let go, even when it seems way too soon. They have taught us that the only thing of permanence in life is love and that to spend life rejoicing in its opportunities and its mystery is better than to spend life adding to its misery and sorrow.

Many a great poet has understood the powerful lessons and blessings in sharing life with an enlightened dog. Lord Byron wrote these words on a monument in tribute to his dog, Boatswain:

> *Near this Spot*
> *Are deposited the Remains of one*
> *Who possessed Beauty without Vanity,*
> *Strength without Insolence,*
> *Courage without Ferocity,*
> *And all the Virtues of Man without his Vices.*[1]

Walt Whitman wrote:

> *I think I could turn and live with the animals, they are so placid and self-contain'd....*
> *They do not sweat and whine about their condition,*
> *They do not lie awake in the dark and weep for their sins ...*
> *Not one is dissatisfied, not one is demented with the mania of owning things.*[2]

---

[1] Lord Byron, "Inscription on the Monument of a Newfoundland Dog: A Memorial to Boatswain," Newstead Abbey, November 30, 1808. Available at http://readytogoebooks.com/LB-dog63htm (accessed October 2006).

[2] Walt Whitman, *Leaves of Grass* (1855; New York: Pocket Books, 2006), 65.

I believe all creatures are God's masterpieces, but I also think most members of the human race could use some spiritual touching up by the artist. Dogs definitely play a part as spiritual messengers to help with that touch-up. Dogs are healers. They are enlightened. They seem to have figured out how to live beautifully so much better than we humans have. While we struggle to figure out why we were put here on Earth, all a dog wants is to love and be loved — a powerful lesson for us all.

— Dr. Bernie S. Siegel, author of *Love, Medicine, and Miracles* and *101 Exercises for the Soul*

HOW THIS BOOK GOT ITS LEGS

We work as publishing professionals and spend each day editing, writing, and selling books, primarily in the areas of self-help, spirituality, and personal growth. The long hours and the hard work are watched, and occasionally commented on, by the two lounging and often lazy office dogs, Basil and Chloe.

At the end of another exhausting day in the world of publishing, we realized that the dogs, relaxed as ever, must have some secret that allowed them to live a life of such ease, pleasure, and fulfillment. We worked; they slept. We worked; they ate. We worked; they lay in the sun and occasionally chased squirrels. The dogs obviously possessed a wisdom that was sadly missing from our own lives.

From that day on, we watched, listened, and gleaned their subtle yet powerful insights on enlightened living. And so this book came into being, chronicling the ancient wisdom formerly only passed down from wise elder dog to puppy.

In Seattle, Zachary Folk, animal photographer extraordinaire and spiritual seeker, was doing essentially the same thing, capturing this canine wisdom through the lens of his camera. When the authors and photographer met while working on another book project, their karmas collided, although, according to Basil and Chloe, there are no coincidences. A book was born — one that transcends time, space, and language barriers.

— Andrea Hurst and Beth Wilson

INTRODUCTION

Enlightenment. Millions of us search for it, study spiritual teachings to find it, read books seeking it, and walk the path toward it. We bend and twist our bodies in yoga classes attempting to stretch our way to an enlightened existence. We sit in rooms with proper feng shui to create tranquility, attempting to meditate our way down the path to a higher existence. We travel the world over to meet and study with great spiritual teachers to understand the secrets of this elusive attainment. We look for the bigger, better, faster answers to the age-old question, What is the purpose of life?

Maybe our eyes should be on the sparrow...or better yet, the schnauzer, dachshund, or German shepherd. Perhaps the real answers are known by the furry four-legged creatures who voraciously wag their tails. Perhaps humankind's best friends are the gatekeepers of life's greatest mystery. That's right: the canine population has the answers to your questions about karma, the Tao, Zen, inner peace, reincarnation, transcendence, and much more. Who knew that the key to enlightenment isn't a secret code or the quiet space between thoughts but is instead a juicy dog bone and a warm bed to sleep on?

Why didn't our canine friends let us know they hold the key? Why have they let us struggle, contort, meditate, and endlessly search for this treasured information? Simple. Up until now they have been watching and waiting for us to recognize that what appears to be canine laziness is in essence their true teaching — to be content and at peace with who we truly are.

The Lazy Dog's Guide to Enlightenment is the result of countless hours of dog watching, walking, feeding, and belly rubbing to unlock the secrets of true nirvana. It will guide you with easy, attainable steps to a higher awareness — and all without leaving your dog's side. This is not another teaching filled with dogma and restrictions but a philosophy that offers an easy, playful answer to the age-old questions of enlightenment.

No longer will humans need to search for insights and direction on this winding path. No longer will poodles, shih tzus, beagles, greyhounds, terriers, and retrievers languish alone and unpetted while their humans are caught up in the meaningless pursuits of the material world. Once we all learn their secrets, no dog will go unrubbed, no puppy will go unloved, and no pooch will be without a smooch or a Scooby snack! Why look any further for spiritual insights? The bark stops here!

The Lazy Dog's Guide to Enlightenment

Approach

your journey

with a

beginner's mind.

Keep your **face to the light** and your **paws** on the ground.

Listening with **compassion** is as **important** as having the right **words**.

When life turns you **upside down,**

be open to **new perspectives.**

Play often,

and never take yourself too seriously.

Admit to your faults: **What's mine** is mine, and **what's yours** is mine too.

Hold tight to life's simple **pleasures.**

Practice the art of the inner bark.

Follow your instincts on the path to **enlightenment,** no matter how **rocky** it gets.

Let peaceful moments rejuvenate you.

Follow your nose —

a good sniff is worth a thousand words.

Open yourself to **spirit**...

and the **answers** will come.

Take time to contemplate the Divine.

Be willing to ask for **forgiveness**.
We all make **mistakes**,

but who we are is not one of them.

Expand your mind: **study** the ancient **sacred** texts.

Love unconditionally.

The **body** is transitory, the **soul** eternal; don't let a few **wrinkles** worry you.

Life passes quickly, so **enjoy** the ride.

Sprawl-asana: the lazy dog's yoga pose.

Own your **Shadow** side,

for it is **always** with you.

Seek truth.

Leave no door unopened…unless it's time to nap.

Your **destination** is not as important as enjoying the **beauty** along the way.

Be open to those who are different; **friendships** come in all shapes and sizes.

If your **direction** seems unclear, pause to **consider** your options.

Embrace your **inner wolf**.

Create good **karma** — channel your frustration into **positive** activities.

In the face of **temptation**, maintain Zenlike **composure**.

(And don't get up unless it's really worth it!)

Establish your **boundaries**

and own your **space**.

Keep an ear out for the **sacred sound**

of the treat jar.

Face up to the things you have to do —
you'll feel better when they're finished.

Retain your puppylike innocence.

Sometimes just
being is enough.

Dive into new experiences. **Looking** back can keep you from **moving** forward.

Believe in **soul mates.**
Love for **one** increases **love for all.**

Chant holy mantras.

Ommm...ownnn...bone...bone...

The quest for **enlightenment**

is only as difficult as you make it:

The **hard** way

or

the **lazy dog** way.

Need a **hug**?

It's okay to ask for and give **affection**.

Be content.

Longing is the root of all suffering.

When your **path** seems **blocked**, have **faith**, and your next **step** will be revealed.

Stretch often:

downward dog pose, ear-to-ground variation.

When you get to the **end** of your **rope**,
it's time to **trust** and **let go**.

Smile! It's the simplest way to **share joy**.

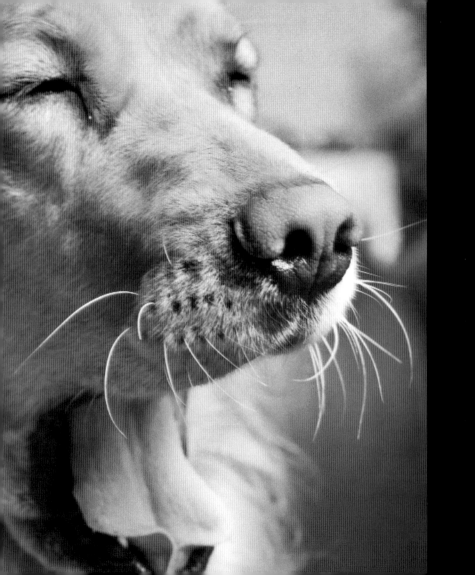

Bark, bark, bark.

Be **discerning** when seeking **wisdom** from higher sources. Some will speak in **tongues**, others in **riddles**.

Have the **patience** to wait.
Right **timing** is everything.

Be slow to **blame** and quick to **forgive**.

Savor the perfection of **All That Is.**

Trust your **intuition**, and invisible **forces** will **guide** you.

Reaching **nirvana** can be as **simple** as surrendering to a **natural high**.

Always remember…

that love is the purpose, the way, and the answer.
It may pop up in the most unlikely places
and occasionally may come with a wet nose.
You deserve love — everyone does.
Our canine best friends
are shining, wriggling,
loyal examples of unconditional love.
Be open to canine wisdom.
Learn to love and be loved.

ACKNOWLEDGMENTS

From the Authors

We would like to thank Basil and Chloe for being constant sources of inspiration while we wrote this book, and our family and friends for their support and good humor.

And to our insightful and canine-friendly editor, Vanessa Brown, we thank you for your steadfast support and the enthusiasm you have brought to this project. To Marc, Kristen, Georgia, Mary Ann, and everyone else at New World Library, thank you for helping to spread the beautiful messages that the animal kingdom has to share.

From the Photographer

Special thanks for the love and support from mom and dad and my wife, Lisa.

ABOUT ANDREA HURST

Andrea Hurst is a literary agent, editor, and author. For more than twenty years, Andrea has worked with many authors in the areas of self-help and spirituality, including bestselling author and animal rights advocate Dr. Bernie Siegel on his award-winning children's book, *Smudge Bunny*. She has been an active supporter of many animal charities, including Best Friends Animal Society and the Humane Society of the United States. Andrea lives in Northern California with her ever-entertaining duo of miniature dachshunds, Basil and Chloe.

ABOUT BETH WILSON

Beth Wilson works with nonprofit organizations doing fundraising, marketing, and program management. For Andrea Hurst Literary Management, Beth works as a developmental editor and book evaluator for authors and publishers. She has a degree in English with a focus on nineteenth-century British literature. Beth lives in Northern California and supports several local animal charities, such as the ASPCA. One of her deepest yearnings is for a little brown Yorkie.

ABOUT ZACHARY FOLK

The work of highly acclaimed Seattle photographer Zachary Folk can be seen in galleries, calendars, product packaging, and advertisements worldwide. His portfolio may be viewed on his website, www.folkphotography.com. He has a passion for travel photography and spends time photographing in Ireland, Vietnam, Thailand, England, and the western United States. When he began to point his lens toward subjects of the canine variety, he found great pleasure and has spent the past several years trying to capture the beauty and wonderful personalities of dogs. He has always had a deep respect and love for all living things, and his educational degrees in wildlife biology and anthropology give him the holistic understanding and perspective needed to see and photograph his subjects. He spends about four months each year doing biological fieldwork, chasing and photographing owls in Northern California.

PLEASE VISIT US AT
www.lazydogsguide.com